Isabelle Hamptonstone MSc.

101

Short Steps to Radiance

A PRACTICAL GUIDE FOR PEACE OF MIND.

Isabelle Hamptonstone MSc.

Isabelle Hamptonstone MSc.

ISBN: 1463712286

ISBN-13: 978-1463712280

Cover design by William Dallimore

The advice in this book is not intended as a substitute for psychological counseling. The author and publisher disclaim any responsibility for liability resulting from actions advocated or discussed in this book.

Isabelle Hamptonstone MSc.

ACKNOWLEDGMENTS

My gratitude to those who have been my inspiration and have provided steadfast support:

Beatrice & Terry Smith, George Buttuls,
Vic Beisel, Karra Farch, Pam Schneider,
Cathy Ferguson, Jes Hynes, Don Arney,
Pat and Heinz Ehlbeck &
William Dallimore.

There's a warm cwtch waiting for you.

Isabelle Hamptonstone MSc.

For Kaz

Isabelle Hamptonstone MSc.

CONTENTS

1. Introduction   1

2. 101 Short Steps   9

3. Further Information   112

4. Results   115

5. Contact   120

"Heaven never helps the man who will not act."

Sophocles

This is a book of action and experience...

Isabelle Hamptonstone MSc.

Your action and experience...

FACT: You are at your most powerful when your mind is clear and focused. You feel more confident, you radiate great energy and you even appear to be more attractive.

When you choose how you use your thoughts, you change how you experience your world.

This book provides you with a simple once a day training to develop a new habit of seeing the world from a brighter, more positive perspective.

The greatest learning in life is often the simplest. However, the seed of learning will only bear fruit when acted upon.

Fortunate are those that know what to do, wise are those who go out and do it.

The key to success is good intention followed by action.

All the wonderful intentions you can ever have carry less weight than one well-meaning action.

Turn your good intentions into actions using this book and experience the reward of training your own brain.

Repetition is the key to producing lasting structural change in the brain. Do anything 101 times and watch that new habit form.

Use one intention for action each morning as a filter through which you experience the rest of your day.

This powerful new habit, repeated daily, will alter you, the energy that you radiate, your perception of your world and your perception of your value within it.

By choosing to train your brain daily you will forever change how you deal with challenging situations. Act on these good intentions and may your radiance shine through all that you do!

Isabelle

Supporting the Sun Peaks School

Part of the proceeds of the sales of book will be donated to the Sun Peaks Education Society Discovery Centre for Balanced Education.

The Centre is a non-profit community charity, which provides community based education in a mountain resort setting where all the young students are inspired to be the best they can be.

www.balancededucation.ca

Isabelle Hamptonstone MSc.

Your 101 Short Steps to Radiance starts right here...

Isabelle Hamptonstone MSc.

Action 1

Feed your mind.

There is a nutrient quality to each word you choose to use. Negative words have a low energy. Positive and inspiring words are far more nutrient rich and replenish your mental energy.

Words are concentrated focusers of energy. Speak well to yourself and others and feed your mental energy today.

Action 2

| + = + |

Our thoughts, feelings, words, actions and energy produce responses, which, in turn, attract similar responses.

Negative responses attract negative responses, and positive responses attract positive responses.

Today, actively attract positive energy into your life with your positive intentions and actions.

Action 3

When we 'try' to do something, it sends a signal to subconscious that there is just as much chance of not doing what we try to do as there is of actually doing it.

As Yoda says, "Do or do not, there is no try."

When you decide to do something today, do it.

Action 4

Did you know that anxiety is one of your greatest tools for success?

Anxiety and negative thoughts
are sharp pokes
from the subconscious mind that tells us
that we are focusing on
what we do NOT want.

Today, use this new perspective on
anxiety to
focus on what it is you DO want.

Action 5

Trying to always please other people is like trying to juggle kittens.

Both tasks leave you physically and mentally drained, and you're end up asking what was the point?!

What other people think of you is not your concern, so today, refocus your mental energy on your goals, rather than on the judgment of those around you.

Action 6

What radio station are you
tuned into today?

Your brain acts as a receiver for exactly
whatever you put your attention to.

Today, practice by seeing how many red
cars you can spot. Then see how many
opportunities to have a good 'belly laugh'
you can find today.

Action 7

Sweat the small stuff!

The more you notice the smallest amounts of happiness the more you will actively experience.

When you experience joy today, hold onto the experience and appreciate it. As you extend your focus, become aware of the surge in your mental energy as your happiness increases.

Action 8

There is an East Indian saying that we are all given a certain number of breaths in this world, and that we are meant to use each one wisely. The worrisome mosquito is in a rush and uses all of his up quickly in a life that lasts a few hours. The elephant is wise in her use of each of her breaths and lives well for a very long time.

Pay attention to your breath today, and take your time enjoying each, peacefully, in turn.

Action 9

Being unique is a quality that comes naturally to you.

Today ask those whom you love and trust what three positive words they would use to describe you.

Listen carefully to their positive responses and focus on your unique qualities today.

Action 10

You were born deserving the best in life.

That hasn't changed. You still do.

Today and everyday, treat yourself with
the respect and kindness
that you deserve.

Action 11

Do each task today with all your heart.

As we say here in my village, Sun Peaks, Giv 'er Balls, (Thanks Bryn!)

If it is a boring job the time will go quicker, you will be more focused, and it will be over before you know it.

Action 12

We connect to our inner wisdom by paying close attention to how we feel.

Every time you feel at ease, you are receiving - without exception - communication from your Higher Self letting you know you are on the right path.

Pay close attention to your decisions today and how you feel when you make them.

Action 13

Retrain Your Focus For Achievement:

Are you appreciating the skill you have as a reader, or maybe the ability you have to use tiny muscles to turn over a page in a book?

If you want more to appreciate, appreciate more what you have right now, in THIS moment.

Action 14

Fear or faith?

Pay attention to your thoughts to become aware and to see if you are acting out of fear or faith.

Today, choose to act out of faith that you can achieve anything you set your mind to.

Action 15

Words have wings to speak good things.

Your kind words act like dropping stones in a pond. They resonate outwards in ever-increasing circles.

Your words may affect a person's life more than you know, so choose your words with wisdom today.

Action 16

How you think and feel draws into your life experiences that match your thoughts and feelings.

The more you focus on your dreams and feel how magnificent it would be the achieve them, the more power you have to manifest them into you own reality.

Think, feel and focus on your dreams today.

Action 17

Notice the conversations around you.

Who is speaking words that inspire you to be greater than you have ever been?

Choose wisely and connect with people who inspire you today.

Action 18

Following on from yesterday's action...Be the person whom you want to connect with.

If you want to be with more inspirational people, be the catalyst for inspiration today.

Action 19

We hear:

"When you need a teacher,
one appears."

The most successful people know when
they need help, and they ask for it.

Today, go straight to those who have
dedicated themselves to their craft, apply
yourself fully to their learning, and
jumpstart your journey to your next level
of personal development.

Action 20

We know that the words 'thank you' are some of the most powerful words that we can use.

Choose today to find many, many ways to feel thankful for what you have and who you are.

Be aware that as you do so, you invite into your life more reasons to be grateful.

Action 21

You have made it this far in life with a great degree of success or else you would not be reading this page right now.

What you get by achieving your goals is not as important as what you become by achieving your goals.

Now show deep appreciation of the skills that you have learned in this lifetime, and put them to good use today.

Action 22

You are the architect of your own life.

You may have a clear blueprint of what you want in life or you may have no idea.

It all starts with just a little imagination.

Today, take a little time to daydream.

Action 23

What is the legacy you want to be remembered for?

Take the time today to consider what you would like your legacy to be.

What do you need to do to achieve this legacy?

Action 24

Energy follows thought.

What you think, you become.

Take the time to consider a good course of action which would help you to achieve your goals today.

Then act.

Action 25

When truly successful people make a mistake they know that they are closer to getting it right next time.

We can all choose to learn from the mistakes we make.

Know today, that making a mistake has helped you to learn and evolve. Your future success depends on you doing so.

Action 26

Doing what you love is very attractive.

Your eyes sparkle, you are happy about life, your joy is infectious.

Focus your energy on doing what makes your heart sing and do what you love today.

Action 27

Random Act of Love and Kindness

You have the ability to influence another person and encourage them to be a greater, more confident version of themselves.

Whose confidence will you increase today with a kind word and complete support?

Action 28

Emotional Intelligence and Empathy.

Until we have a walked a mile in another person's shoes, how can we really know what they have been experiencing?

Judgment of others can only come from a place of 'not knowing'. Choose today to refocus your mental energy on your goals and dreams, and fuel your own success.

Action 29

By removing the energy drains in your life you create the space for positive opportunities to come to you.

What small, everyday occurrences are 'bugging you' and are draining your mental energy?

Today, identify and release 10 energy drains in your life.

Action 30

"Praise you like I should." Fatboy Slim

Positive reinforcement is the key to encouraging great behavior.

Take time to praise the great effort of those around you and in doing so, encourage them to do more of the same.

Action 31

Every person who has come onto this earth deserves to be appreciated.

You especially do.

From the smallest appreciation comes an increase in happiness, peace and success.

Look for every opportunity to appreciate yourself.

Action 32

Learning to catch.

Sometimes the world throws us a curve ball, and then we realize that was exactly what we needed to learn how to catch.

Today, appreciate that the curve balls you field today will help you win the game in the long run.

Action 33

Out of bounds?

A boundary simply defines what people can and cannot do to you.

If a person does not respect your boundaries, that is their choice.

Today, take the time to decide what, for you, are your deal breakers.

Action 34

In every conversation we take one of three roles.

We can dictate
(similar to how a parent would with a child),
we can be submissive
(just like a child will often be to a parent), or
we can take the role of the adult
(and stand quietly grounded).

Notice today the role you take in your conversations. Parent, Adult, Child?

Action 35

I cannot stress this enough:

The greatest gift you can give the world is to take excellent care of yourself.

So, once again, remind yourself that finding time for your pleasure is the easiest way to nourish yourself.

The more you take care of yourself, the more your ability to care for others increases.

Action 36

Two of the most powerful words used as personal descriptions are:

Honor and Integrity.

Complete the smallest of tasks today with good intent and honor. The immediate and eventual rewards will be fully justified.

Action 37

Inspiration and you.

Being your best serves as an example to others and encourages them to shine and do the same.

Provide inspiration to others today with your thoughts and deeds.

Action 38

You and I are like teabags.

Often we don't know how strong we are until we are put into hot water!

In the midst of our greatest challenges we have the opportunity to realize our personal power.

Identify your personal strength in response to a challenge today.

Action 39

"With all I have I say Thank You".

Counting your blessings opens up your subconscious to more experiences to bless.

Start the day by listing 10 of the things you are most grateful for.

Action 40

Be infectious!

Here's what I mean...A smile, like a yawn, is infectious!

Who will you infect with a heartfelt smile today?

Action 41

Your immune system eavesdrops on pictures, sounds and memories that you hold in your head.

Think well, be well.

Nurture your body with the finest foods, and nurture your mind with the kindest thoughts about yourself today.

Action 42

We all have the ability to become dragged down by the ebb and flow of life.

We all have the ability to take learning from the ebb and flow to propel us onto our next journey.

Choose to learn from your experiences today and propel yourself along to the next great goal.

Action 43

The simplest way to self-nourish...

Gently become aware of your breath and, as you do, send an intention of deep and powerful relaxation to every single cell of your body.

Action 44

You will seek what you are determined to find.

There is something special to be found in the darkest of days if you are convinced that you are going to find it.

Decide, right now, what type positive experience you want to find in this day, and then find it.

Action 45

Power up.

Our power comes from a willingness to honor our ability to make ourselves happy.

Today, act in the knowledge that the responsibility for your happiness is completely yours.

Action 46

The secret to great relationships?
Deep ease, deep ease, deep ease.

Relationships thrive when they are born
out of deep ease.

Who will you make a new and easy
friendship with today?

Action 47

The most successful people I know choose to learn 3 positive lessons from each challenging situation that they face

It allows them to make the most of what they are presented with and to focus on moving forward toward their personal goals.

What positive learnings will you take from a challenge today?

Action 48

To be enlightened is to lighten up.

My favorite advice from the Maharishi Mahesh Yogi is to

"Stay childlike."

He knew a thing or two about sustaining his own happiness...!

What positive child-like trait will you choose to use today?

Action 49

We all develop our emotional tools daily, with our action and experience.

We all learn new skills every day.

Know that any challenge you face today will provide you with the opportunity to develop those tools and skills.

Action 50

When you get caught up in thinking about the things you feel you cannot do, remember there once was a time when you could not hold a book, read a page or write your own name.

Your list of achievement is lengthy, and it is only natural that this list will grow longer today. What will you do today that will add to your list?

Action 51

Visualization is even more powerful when we combine thoughts and feelings to become mighty manifestors.

Power up the visual by taking 10-15 minutes imagining what you would see, hear, feel, taste and smell when you have achieved what you want to achieve.

This gives your subconscious a clearer and more powerful prescription for accomplishing your goals.

Action 52

Your need for gentle care is as strong as the need you had when you were first born. The difference is that, now, you can provide that gentle care for yourself.

Today, treat yourself with the same love and attention to your own needs that you would a newborn.

Action 53

Perception IS projection.

Today, look for three different perspectives on one situation.

Take on the role of the observer and develop your emotional intelligence.

Action 54

If your heart and soul sing with joy, then your choice is a right one.

If they do not, then find a choice that makes it so.

Today, choose with wisdom.

Action 55

Tidy house, tidy mind.

Your outside space is a projection of
your inner space.

Today clear at least one item from your
house or in storage
that you no longer need.

Action 56

Dream daily.

"Imagination is more important than knowledge." Albert Einstein.

Take time today to close your eyes, open your mind and imagine. Let your imagination take you far beyond your wildest, happiest dreams and set in place the first steps to manifesting your daydreams.

Action 57

Happiness is the consequence of personal effort. It is a task that one actively participates in.

Does anyone tell you happiness is all in the mind? That's where it starts.

Now go and do something healthy that makes you happy.

Now

Action 58

Its that time again, time for a clean up.

If you are serious about being successful, start by getting rid of those small annoyances that you are putting up with.

Everything you are tolerating drains your personal power.

Clear Up, Power Up.

Action 59

You are what you think.

So, are you lucky or unlucky?

Either way, you will ultimately find what you seek.

What will you, in this moment, choose to be for the rest of your day?

Action 60

Your beauty shines through your words, thoughts and actions.

Beauty is as beauty does.

Choose your actions today that will reveal your inner beauty today.

Action 61

Do you ever feel shy accepting a compliment?

The skill is in accepting
the verbal gift offered to you.

If you don't know quite what to say, just quietly say 'thank you' and, with gentle acceptance, acknowledge the gift received.

Action 62

Steer your own ship by paying attention to your emotions.

Is there more room for laughter and positivity?

Then today, navigate towards the people who laugh with open and kind hearts.

Action 63

Situations change daily.

What we can experience today we will never get to experience in the same way again.

Adore what you do today whilst you still get to do it.

Action 64

How's your energy today?

We already know that doing what you love replenishes your energy.

Choose actions that Recharge you today.

Action 65

Thinking, doing, being, experiencing.

Reading about being calm and peaceful is the start. Now walk your walk and look for those tiny gems of calm and peace in your day today.

Action 66

"Everyone has a spirit that can be refined, a body that can be trained in some manner, a suitable path to follow.

You are here to realize your inner divinity and manifest your innate enlightenment."

Morihei Ueshiba

Action 67

In the words of Buddha, "If you cannot find the truth right where you are, where else do you think you will find it?"

We can look and try to find the answer to our problems in our surroundings, in our families, in our workplace. We can travel many miles to find ourselves, yet we always take ourselves along.

Today, decide that how you feel is your responsibility.

Action 68

Failure does not make or break you.

What is important is how you choose to react to failure.

Today, once again choose to see your challenges as training for your next success.

Action 69

The subconscious mind records every
single thing that we experience.

All too often we look back at a situation
and know that we could,
with hindsight, have experienced it in a
totally different way if we had had a
different frame of mind.

In what frame of mind will you choose
to experience your life today?

Action 70

Experience and reinforce.

There will be some person or situation that will make you smile today.

Focus and experience the good feeling until it intensifies throughout your whole body as you unite body and mind and strengthen your neural pathways to happiness.

Action 71

Be the driving force behind your own good mood.

If you want more laughter in your life, decide to find ways to be fun to be around.

Plan to bring joy and laughter into another person's life today and watch the ripples of happiness flow back to you.

Action 72

Ever think to yourself ... I will know when I'm successful when (this) happens?

Know that your day has already been full of success. List your successes so far in this day and stop when you get to 20.

If you want to be more successful, begin by recognizing the success in each moment.

Action 73

Control of your ability to relax starts with noticing and gently guiding your thoughts. It is by being mindful that we move from being the pawn onto the chessboard to being the chess grandmaster, and we begin to see ourselves in control.

Choose to think gently and mindfully today. As you do so, you invite relaxation into your world.

Action 74

Humans are creatures of habits

We are told that it takes courage to make the first step.

Once you have thought of what you can do, the first step has already taken place.

What first steps will you take today towards making new powerful and positive habits?

Action 75

Did you know that the mind can only think one thought at a time?

What you choose to focus on affects your ability to be calm, focused and relaxed.

Which thoughts will you choose to focus more time on today?

Action 76

Who are you? You decide.

> "There are three kinds of people. Those who makes things happen, those who watch things happen, and those who ask what happened?!"
>
> Wilf Bennett, Sun Peaks.

Who will you choose to be today?

Action 77

Be present, not absent.

How?

Focus your attention completely on exactly what it is you are doing right in this moment. Start with holding that attention for 10 seconds.

Right here, right now, all is good.

You are present.

Action 78

As you have been working through this book day by day you will have experienced a shift in awareness.

Just the slightest opening of awareness can cause a shift in how you experience the world. As we become more aware of the impact of our thoughts on our lives, reality has already shifted.

Today, note the positive changes that have taken place over the last 77 days.

Action 79

"Today I can complain because the weather is rainy or I can be thankful that the grass is getting watered for free."

Author Unknown

In NLP what we have here is a simple reframe. A reframe is a filter through which we can chose to find limitations or opportunity in each situation that we face. Today, reframe, reframe and reframe and train your brain to identify more opportunities for health and happiness.

Action 80

Today reinforce your training so far:

We can gently and quickly become aware and train our minds to have pre chosen expectations.

Today, have the expectation of finding peace in the simplest of tasks and simplicity in the most peaceful of moments.

Action 81

Your internal guidance system, how you feel, is the most reliable measure of how well you are living your life.

Our internal guidance systems provide us with a sense of direction.

Today, listen to your feelings quietly and carefully and use them to find your own True North.

Action 82

Look to connect with the people who have what you want.

When you see others achieve the goals that you long to achieve, smile and know that if they can, so can you.

Delight in the successes of others.

They are your inspiration.

Action 83

You are your own creation.

There are many ways to be creative.

Write, draw, sing, think, speak in a way that you have never before.

Today, create.

Action 84

The power of intent.

Your gentle heart can impact another person's life in ways we may never fully comprehend.

Today, reconnect with an old friend to share your warmth and steadfast support.

Action 85

The danger of assumption.

The tricky part about assuming motive or intention is that we will never ever be able to see the world through the eyes of another person.

Take the time today to communicate and find the courage to ask gentle questions to develop your own understanding of another person's point of view.

Action 86

Remember that the best way to take care of others is to take the greatest care of yourself.

Each time you take better care of yourself, you improve your state of mind, and this has a **positive impact** on how you **perceive** the world around you.

Today create a better world by taking gentle and excellent care of yourself.

Action 87

When you commit to a plan and act upon it, the energy of your actions brings unforeseen reward.

Today,

Think, commit, and act.

Action 88

We are the directors and producers of the movies that play in our mind.

You can choose to watch a horror show, a comedy or the inspirational story of your life.

Today, become aware of which TV channel you are choosing to watch.

Action 89

Time to Replenish

Smile gently, and send that gentle smile to every cell in your system.

The endorphins will flow with your intention to replenish yourself spiritually, mentally, physically and emotionally.

Action 90

Attract the ideal person by being the
ideal person.

If you want good friends, be a good
friend. If you want a warm spirited
partner, be warm spirited.

Use this technique today to actively
draw into your life those whom you feel
would enhance it.

Action 91

Energy follows thought. The more energy you apply to a thought in the form of action, the more powerful a manifestor you will be.

Take the time to consider what would be a good course of action, which would help you to achieve your goals today. Then act.

Action 92

Having affection, feeling accepted and feeling appreciated are examples of important needs.

The more conscious you become of what your needs are, the more creative you will become in finding ways to meet those needs.

Take the time today to consider what your needs are and begin to fulfill those needs yourself.

Action 93

We have heard that we should dance like
no one's watching;
Act like no one's judging!

All too often our fear of the judgment of others makes us stop in our tracks and steer away from achieving our greatest desires.

Know that today, whatever you decide to do with a good heart will be fully supported by somebody, somewhere.

Action 94

The most powerful clients that I have trained know that they are finally strong enough to show their weakness.

It takes an incredibly strong person to show that they too, sometimes, need support.

Today, when you need it, ask for help.

Action 95

The more relaxed we are, the more powerful we become.

Choose today to notice when you act from a mindspace of relaxation, how easily you can achieve your goals.

Action 96

Be diligent with your thoughts and your words. The lens through which we see the world shapes our reality.

When we change how we speak to ourselves and others, we can change the outcome of how we relate to ourselves and others.

Today, speak with kindness and respect, to yourself.

Action 97

The mind and the body manifest expression from the same single system. If you are feeling uncomfortable, then you are thinking uncomfortable thoughts. 'Every man is what he is because of the dominating thoughts which he permits to occupy his mind.' Napoleon Hill

Monitor your thoughts today and carefully choose the subjects that you choose to dwell upon.

Action 98

How we speak to others is often how we speak to ourselves.

Today, develop a greater understanding of your family members, your work colleagues and team members by listening carefully to how they speak to others, it tells you so much about how they speak to themselves.

Action 99

Ever have that chattering monkey on your shoulder that gives you a running commentary on how well you're not doing?

Here's where we come full circle, the chattering monkey is reminding us that we are focusing on the negative. When I hear him chatter away now, I thank him for letting me know that I can choose to refocus my headspace.
Just for today, thank your monkey!

Action 100

> 'What progress, you ask, have I made?
> I have begun to be a friend to myself.'
>
> Hecato.

The greatest friendship you will ever develop is the one you have with yourself.

Today, acknowledge 3 ways in which your relationship with yourself has been improved, since we began this journey together, 100 days ago.

Action 101

Your very first intention and action was to use this book for your self development. Your skill and ability to train your own brain has been developed in response to the actions that you have taken over the last 100 days.

Today, seek to connect with other people that also see the world from a brighter, more positive perspective...

And shine...!

ABOUT BRAIN TRAIN
INTERNATIONAL

COMPANY VISION

Brain Train International is
dedicated to connecting
with the highest self of
every person on the planet to
positively impact
their perception of the world and
their value within it.

ABOUT THE AUTHOR

Isabelle Hamptonstone is a Neuro Linguistics Programming Consultant, Hypnotherapist, Transcendental Meditator, Award Winning Sports Instructor and the founder of Brain Train International.

Isabelle has lived in Sun Peaks, Canada, for a decade and loves to ski those beautiful bluebird B.C. days, especially when Wales win the rugby!

"Your State of Mind is the key to winning and is fundamental to your ever increasing success. If I can help one person to see how radiant and powerful they actually are, my heart is happy."

Isabelle Hamptonstone 2011

Isabelle Hamptonstone MSc.

Having Izzy as my NLP consultant has transformed me. I am now a more grounded and powerful competitor.

Elli Terwiel,
World Cup Ski Team, Canada

Izzy has had a great impact on my life and I would recommend her to anyone who is seriously looking to make positive steps in their personal and financial life. I feel so confident with her services that I would give you your money back, if you were not completely satisfied. I will never be able to thank you enough Izzy! I feel amazing. I feel much focused towards the future. I want to be able to share this with people that come into my life that are looking for it.

Parker Bennett, Entrepreneur

Ms. Hamptonstone has consistently provided inspiration and a pathway of training to a 'healthy mind'.

**George Buttuls (Cst.),
Royal Canadian Mounted Police**

I have now conquered major personal and sports goals that I have been working on for the past 5 years.

Brett Dawley, Professional Skier

Isabelle has customized a program for me and has helped me turn possibilities into realities.

Eric Manion, Manager

Isabelle's ability to manage complex issues gives her an edge as an NLP Consultant.

**Cathy Ferguson RN, BScN
Clinical Practice Educator – Psychiatry**

Izzy has a big heart and loves people. She is always looking for more within herself to develop others in terms of personal evolution.

Don Arney, Owner SEI Industries

I work with Izzy about twice a month and I wake up feeling different, I feel amazing. How I'm experiencing my life has changed, it has turned around. I have lot to give this world and now I feel I am connected to my confidence and resources.

Jodi Moar

Isabelle lives into the standards of excellence and walks her talk. I was amazed and delighted by her insight, humor and high capability in the field of NLP.

Donna Fleetwood, Realtor

Working with Izzy as my NLP consultant has been one of the single most beneficial experiences I have ever had. I have achieved confidence in myself as well as my abilities. I have accomplished many goals in such a short period of time and couldn't be happier.

Marlie Marchewka,
Pro Snowboarder

Izzy provides a safe and comforting environment that allows her clients to express concerns that are both readily apparent as well as deeply rooted.

Denise Mahon,
University of Victoria

Isabelle is highly intuitive, very professional yet easy to relate to. I have found each session to be very full and rewarding and would not hesitate to recommend her services.

Dana Lacroix, Artist

In competitive 4-Cross and Downhill Mountain Bike racing, you have to be very focused and goal oriented to win. I found this to be in the forefront of Izzy's sessions. Working with Izzy has helped me to develop a winning attitude. As a professional businessman, working with Izzy is also helping me to manifest my own personal goals. The passion and understanding for her clients and subjects she coaches is second to none. I could not think of a better person to help me in my sport, business and life.

Kurt Wolf,
Elite Mountain Bike Racer

With Izzy's help I have become a more confident competitor who is ready to tackle whatever lies ahead in regards to ski competitions AND everyday life. Izzy has brought out the best in me.

Emma Whitman,
Professional Skier

Izzy Hampton Stone is a person who believes in maximizing each person's potential through retraining the brain's way of thinking. She has helped successful athletes, and business owners and she can help you too!

If you are ready for more of Izzy's help. Simply go to her website: www.btmvp.com or email her isabelle@btmvp.com and experience all the ways she can help you to think in new ways to change how you concentrate your thoughts, maximize the extraordinary in all things, big or small, and help you to make life change that will create a confident, successful and peaceful life.

SPORT BUSINESS

BRAINTRAIN
INTERNATIONAL
250-320-7047 btmvp.com

TRAIN YOUR BRAIN
TO WIN

13008725R00084

Made in the USA
Lexington, KY
09 January 2012